PETER ARMSTRONG

RISINGS

ENITHARMON PRESS 1988

First published in 1988
by the Enitharmon Press
40 Rushes Road
Petersfield
Hampshire GU32 3BW

© Peter Armstrong

Cover design by Noel Connor

ISBN 1 870612 00 0

This publication
is supported
by Northern Arts

The Enitharmon Press acknowledges financial
assistance from Southern Arts

Set in Monotype 12 point Bembo (270)
by Gloucester Typesetting Services
and printed by
Antony Rowe Limited, Chippenham, Wiltshire

CONTENTS

Borderers 9
Songs at Birtley 10
Pit Lines 11
A Metamorphosis 12
Three Pennine Poems 13
Idle 16
On the Eve of Signing 18
The Inheritors 20
Another Company 22
A Song against Winter 23
Grey Heroes 25
A Song for Harry Lime 26
Barabbas 27
Barabbas, in the Cells, to Jesus 29
Barabbas, in his Old Age, to Jesus 30
Barabbas in his Kingdom 31
The Book of Acts 32
Barabbas Carves his Headstone 33
Quick! The Serum! 34
Cybermen 35
For Jim Deighan 37
In Memoriam John McGurk 39
Her Rosary 40
I See Myself in the Womb 41
A Song for the Faithful Departed at the Winter Solstice 43
A Deaf Woman in her Old Age 44
The Resurrection of the Dead 45
Tollesbury 46
Keeping Silence 47
A Song at Four A.M. 48
Promised Land 49
A Gift of Healing 50
Silent Ancestry 52

We look for the resurrection of the dead,
and the life of the world to come.

ACKNOWLEDGEMENTS

Acknowledgement is due to the editors of the following anthologies and periodicals in which some of these poems have appeared:

10 North East Poets (Bloodaxe 1980), New Poetry 7 (Hutchinson/Arts Council), The Gregory Poems 1983-84 (Salamander/Society of Authors), New Angles II (Oxford University Press), Poetry Review, Other Poetry, Here Now, North, Outposts, Stand.

Grateful thanks to all who have assisted the author's writing over the past ten years, especially Roger Garfitt, Richard Kell, the literature department of Northern Arts, and members of Sunderland Polytechnic writers' workshop 1977-80.

BORDERERS

Imagine land of lank grasses,
of acid soil fixed kingdoms gutter on
where the honed wind sounds
the wire's harmonic
                        and the mind opens
on long marches, a cadence of fells
beneath the mist's bled flank
and further back
in momentary focus, riders
close to ground.

They are moth against bark,
bracken's geometry,
lichen on stone crosses,
mind brooding on morphology.

Hedging bloodfeud, bordering
the dumb wound of moor
they are adrift among nations, a people
at the mind's turning
                        entering
on grey; the bearing of their voices lost
beneath the wind's sloughed locutions.

And if mist rises
see them here
between washed skies
and the rivers' absolution

hinged on nothing
– that filament of cirrus
light animates.

SONGS AT BIRTLEY

Listen how the voices go; a light step
on the threshold, a sure foot
on known soil.

Tonight we walk the hinterland, the common places
where the hills might burn, our eyes settle
on a particular wilderness. The room has given

on a bright familiar vision: we bow
as men praying.
And one rises:

a low voice sounding levels, mapping out
the buried ground. Drowned chambers
surface in his song, his brow furrows

to a white field of histories:
the tribe swells in the chorus. And we
are the refrain of the dead

who rise to meet us in the outlying towns,
silhouettes in the low sun's corona,
open-handed. His silence is their going

– and the terraces slew over into night.
Wires shudder: gables slip. The birds return
to a cracked street, insurgent grass in the doorways

that murmurs
               a rising in the dark,
a lilt in the fields, a phrase in the wind.
Above the bowed villages the night long

this calling-over, a singing line.

PIT LINES

    were silence tending fallow ash
        and bramble, an absence spanning hollow chambers
           thin voices flickered through

    where beds of nettle washed
        against fractured brick, and the drift
           was shadow in the kingdom of fern.

In the leaf's turning,
    in the root's thrust through concrete
        long exile ended,

in the memory of seed;
    this joining in the bread
        and berry of reunion. But we

born into the long shade
    hope only to come from clinging growth
        upon the lost and narrowing black path

to feel underfoot the saddle of ash
    between prints of sleepers
        and come at last

beyond slag's Akeldama to where
    half-fallen cathedrals of white brick
        have made us a brotherhood

with bindweed and willow-herb;
    unremarkable, but sure inheritors
        of the vacant kingdom.

A METAMORPHOSIS

Hearing the earth move above him
   and split along its memory of grain
   he could only raise one
whitefleshed, blackgrained arm

to the oncoming roof,
   as if to reach air with it,
   narrowing his hand to a leaf, regret
of the dark and the stiff

tree of his genealogy honing
   to a white shaft
   that now, a season after,
has broken ground, bending

to the open weather, a hand
   opening its thank-offering
   to air, lifting
a prayer from the black ground.

THREE PENNINE POEMS

1: *Another Ice Age*

As frost forms its fern on glass
  so stone splays its fingers
    through valleys, clings
like lichen to the fell's grey mass

– a glacial age
  played backwards at double
    speed, jerking uphill
its stone thrust, its spillage

of alluvium. Quarries pock hillsides,
  the roads' striations straggle
    drab fields. But the glare
of horizontal sun at valley heads

is the unglaciated plain
  where no erratic fell,
    no masonry stole
hold on moor; the Zion

of strands dissolved, all promises
  come in one last confluence
    together, a brilliance
distilled in the sky's chalice.

2: Rains

Every blackened chapel yields its chiselled praises:
   harvest of the redbrick missions,
   flints of worship, faint incisions
in the faultless basalt face

of a theology. The faith retains
   a footing in the thin earth
   of hilltowns, brings forth
the blunt masonry of creeds among rains

that slant across our knowledge.
   And over the grass on blank slopes
   dry walls of dogma step
towards the millstone tops, the ridges

whose off-cast screes rain down
   shivered flints like an offering
   refused. Above, unseen birds sing
and the ravellings of cloud are undone.

3: A Skyline with no Features

The towns edge up the valley floor
    their blackened sandstone yarn.
  Higher, the peaty water of tarns,
the ruffled expanse of reservoirs

constitute an unpeopled
    nation. Grey windblown grasses
    overlook the terraces
that nuzzle the lowest moors. The Babel

of mills has not dissected the wind's tongue
    here. Its long syllable
    scythes the heather's stubble:
the burnt moor lies beneath its song.

Stand here before the icon of silence;
    the litanies of curlew
    and lapwing strew
random utterance across dissolving tenses

and the wind is gathering to itself
    each reiteration of breath,
    each little recurring Lethe
into its vast fathering gulf.

IDLE

A nettle twines
around the fence's mesh

guarding vacancies;
the arid light

of loading bays,
the foreign quiet

of darkened shop-floors.
At each town's edge

circumscribed by silence
or sidings' ash

empty zones
accumulate.

Where the klaxon sounded
only wind through wire:

an idle summons,
a memory.

5pm, and the empty shops
are yielding

almost transparent men.
They are the dust

of unused warehouses,
the flaked rust

of corrugated walls.
Light ignores them.

Where they emerge
the concrete yards

like chalk
are crumbling.

ON THE EVE OF SIGNING

This winter's mornings we have gathered
with our few words
and our pared-down manner

waiting at the door of the grey basilica,
observing its etiquette,
hugging the wall.

Here and here only
are we known. We meet each other's eye
as a mirror's:

we speak the Esperanto
of the alien. The street
is another country.

If you follow us, it will be as our ghost;
already where your body was
the sun slants through smoke.

Soon we will have forgotten you,
turning our faces to the glass,
knowing that

only the forms are real here,
their measures set
in a slow mime. Our footfalls

become their instances.
Through long corridors
we perfect their patterns

to emerge nameless,
our faces worn smooth
at glass partitions

cradling, like something living,
our rags of ID and claims
– which we lift to you now

being speechless, being without number.
And look: they are fingered white
and supple as linen

and where they catch on a turn of the air
hang and fall leafwise
and for a space

edge with light
perfected and temporary
anonymous as the unborn

THE INHERITORS

Where you would not come;
under arches, by uneven steps,
to this cul-de-sac.

Where you would not come
but as one of this company
in the penumbra

stand aside and look:

light is a crescent on a shoulder,
a grain in the steam from an urn,
a halo over a turned face.

Or listen:

low talk of low things,
hand-outs and cheap lunches,
shelters and promised money.

The calculus earths here.
These are the product of the equations.

Moss on the stones of a city,
unassuming, unseen:

skipping or sifting home
with their bags of bread
and good grace

you would not know them
– Matty, Bobby, Peter, Jon –

keeping their long companionships
or their long solitudes

their genius for survival

all the inheritors
picked out in a sharp light,
then gone

into an interim kingdom.

ANOTHER COMPANY

We are drunk
with Malory

beguiled by Scott
and Spenser.

An ill-focused age
glimmers:

the image
never sharpens

beyond Coeur-de-Lion.

———

But now
I see another company

stragglers from
their masters' wars,

barely visible
above the skyline.

The foreground
diminishes.

The lists are
abandoned

to a grey column
that does not advance.

A SONG AGAINST WINTER

Ash: a fleck that settles
on the brow; a white leaf
brushes at your hand.

As if from a neighbour's bonfire
you turn your shoulder

from a dry fall
drifting in the webs of your fingers,
the fissures of your lips

until ash
is a flesh, and breath
an abrasion in the throat.

Against light's weathering, against
the shrunk mercury, here is a memory
I have cupped in my hands;

you may feel
the small shock of its warmth
or look close

where small figures gather
to a broad field.
The sun is on their backs:

there is a song the wind gathers
and scatters in the shadow of a furrow.

―――

Look now across the length
of foraging months
in a lean light:

a thinned fellowship stooped
to a thin harvest, a song
that catches in the ash of the throat.

Skin flakes its leaves
from the ash brow. Snow powders
a grey soil

and the root we grub for lies
a nail's breadth
from the split nail.

Rags on the black land.
Rags in the black wind, we might
catch on an eddy of the wind;

minutiae in a broad field
flecked with rags.

GREY HEROES

Boots that suck from logged earth. Prints that fill.

Across a meadow pocked with sky
the columns form, lodged
in the middle distance: a drift of grey
between the eye and the mind's
touch; a rumour of an army
gone to ground in the woods.

Hush now as they go among the trees
pliant as cattle, knowing
as the malleable land. Their uniforms
are another skin, their looks
a tacit sabotage, wisdom of the other runners.
Theirs is the patience of the gene:

theirs is the penance of the seed
who have gone into the dark;
a shimmer of grey in the roadways,
no mention in dispatches
– of this other company,
of their episodes in decline, of orders lost, battalions

crossing in the night; of these
who stand at the circles' edges, onlookers
at the counsels, their breaths
rising like the herds', their speech
a compound murmur; whose absence is a whisper
– a hiss in the air where sound should be.

There are so many of that company now.
I see them wade knee-deep through the reeds
at lakesides, coming from the shadows under conifers
into the mind's expanse, its convalescence.
Look where the grass invades the gun-tracks
and the earth gives absolution.

A SONG FOR HARRY LIME

In that last hour, Harry,
did you see yourself becoming icon,
canonized in black gaberdine,
a moment's attitude of prayer towards
the Danube's fenced-off, beatific light?

The fall of rain, the sewers filling,
forced higher in the labyrinth
towards a predetermined meeting:
did you see, Harry, your hands surface
– fingers splayed and supplicant –

as the world tensed in one last spasm
of wars, markets, occupations?
You have become our patron now.
Metaphysics crumble under
your raised eyebrow, your weary shrug.

And through the night
black-marketeers go running
over bomb-sites. We speak three languages
understanding none. Your face presses at our windows
half-seen through traceries of rain.

BARABBAS

We have not named him yet.
We dare not name him.

His has been the footfall on perimeters,
the voice behind flashlights.
We have seen his face as a blur
at midnight, his fist an impact
on our thin doors. He is moving in the dark tonight,
is a hunched presence
in the alleys, a quick shadow

among demolitions. Yet he is the man
of the majority: did he come to the balcony
to be blessed or to bless? To be taken
to the heart. Hero in the daylight, beloved
in the press of hands, he has made his home
on the waste ground, and the people go
in droves to be fed there.

Only in our dreams have we seen him
come into his kingdom; the fences shudder
in the wind's heave where we probe the singing mesh
with numb fingers. When we hear another's voice
it is his, saying gently that
there is no-one there, disentangling our hands
as deftly as a mother might, and is gone.

He is at the border now; he has always been:
we have seen him dimly there
or from a distance. Only at the last
did we recognise the hunched frame, the face
turned at last towards us.
Only as he crossed the suburbs at nightfall
did we put names to him

turning their promise like bread
in our mouths, a kingdom on the lips,
the tongue's epiphany. Only in the bright coal's
touch on the lips did the vision break
of a hand stretched out to bless
or stroke
        and enter.

BARABBAS, IN THE CELLS, TO JESUS

Brother, you will always lose.
I would stretch a hand to you
but cannot reach your loss.
Here, today, between the crevassless law
and the glass-faced faultless multitude,
you will be strung on a thread.

Did you require this circus? Playing
to any house, you declined the heroic,
the tragic posture; danced to your daddy, sang
for everyone else's supper. The slick
occupants of the grand circle
coughed: the gods were equivocal.

And now, down at heel and stage centre,
dyskinesic marionette among deities
and small fry, will you disinter
our closet skeletons? (It is
the clown's function.) Will you exorcise
our deep ghosts, your clown's face

lifted, clear and spot-lit
in a dark altitude?
The crowd have paid for it.
And for me? Had you pursued
our pantomime's logic, you'd have
inferred my exit, saviour,

seen your body bridge
my void, and I, perfect escapologist,
tiptoe across without thanks or grudge,
the crowd beautifully aghast.
Your side breaks at the touch of my instep.
Tense, O my brother, while I make my escape.

BARABBAS, IN HIS OLD AGE, TO JESUS

Brother, there was style in your silence.
When they cried for me
I felt all God running in my veins;
but yours was the perfect policy:
without a turn of the head
you undercut all that was signed or said.

The pity then that you should lose
in pain that perfect pose.
I would have followed but for that.
I can picture you now, lying in state,

though all the time these agents come
carrying their flawed intelligence.
In the elevated cruciform night I dream
of risings and lakeside reunions.

Who is this between the sun and me?
open-handed, choices hanging at his fingers
where the spray lifts from a fish-jammed sea
and the trawlermen sit a while and sing.

BARABBAS IN HIS KINGDOM

Someone is shifting in the rubble,
bent-backed, going almost
on his knuckles
          and straightens
only to sniff the wind, or peer
over the swept acres of his state.

He is marking the borders, pissing
on the brick cairns, howling
from the banks' cracked parapets
across the land's vacuum
                whether now
beneath a glacial sky; or now

his voice a breathcloud
on the night's acid clarities.
He is perfect here; he has found
his niche:
          to see him stand
erect at the city limits, brow knit

over a massive quiet
                and falling
quiet, turning in the evening
for homeplace, mumbling
a snatch of song.
              Come nearer
where he pauses on the boulevard

to sift the refuse with his clever
animal fingers
              chanting softly to himself
rags and bones
          as if it were a lullaby

rags and bones
rags and bones

THE BOOK OF ACTS

    He would not leave them comfortless.

    Gathered in conspiratorial attics
    they signed his name
    and waited for a sign
                    while a kingdom
    encroached on their vision, a blur
    at the eye's margin
                    that grew inwards.
    Light tunnelled it, then lapsed.

    Pinched-faced apostles, walking close to the wall
    they spread the word in whispers,
    eyes narrowed
                  on a city of conduits
    and half-lit subways: murmuring companies
    in a web of tunnels. Its corridors
    spidered into scrub.

    They raised their arms to its coming.

    And in the furnace with them, at the turn
    of the screw, when the trapdoor snapped ajar

    always a voice as heard through tunnels,
    its words wrapped in its echoes
    but unmistakable.
                    They died in ecstasy
    having seen his salvation.

BARABBAS CARVES HIS HEADSTONE

    Keeper of borders
    Oracle of kingdoms
      Whisperer

Whose rest is the scorched earth
      & hope

  that the earth's mills raise
  his perennial convolvulus

QUICK! THE SERUM!

It is one thing, one action quick
and definitive that will save
the world. There is one hero,
one eccentric scientist
who has known all along.

There is one obstacle,
one guffawing baddie
who will come unstuck, one enigma
solved with an 'Of course!'
in the last instalment.

There is one place, one clearing
where the plot unravels, and the cast
come tumbling one behind the other
from the trees with 'There you are!'
and 'We thought you were dead!'.

But nobody is dead
and every casualty will rise
at one snap of the fingers, and death
done out of its dominion
shuffles off one step beyond

the bright ring of cameras.

CYBERMEN

Like every image of the perfect race
they walk imperfectly,
stepping from the brain's blueprint
uneasy with the habitat of space, bodies
stiff as syllogisms, aching
for the abstract.

These are the storm-troopers
of the intellect,
the rational static of their voices
crackling with dicta, cocksure
of their impending millennium, its exact dimensions,
its limpid city

spiralling to earth
under white light. But the page
is their environment; irrational landscapes
open at the feet of gangways,
asymmetric suburbs; in the distance
ash-hills, ghosts of smoke;

and the mutants: rumours out beyond
the dead zones, accidental figures
at the skyline, with their
random language, with their
other Kingdom. The calculations start to go awry:
already contact with the source is lost,

and the blurred print of resistance
shimmers in their field of vision, scrambling
the formulae. Truth-tables
jangle in their heads. Their words
degrade to morse stutters.
From that furthest point

of their advance, that front where
the blank face looked on tundra
they recoiled, reeling-in
each step from first principles,
picked off one by one
before they ever reached the city,

ever saw the silver ship,
and a course projected
across perfect formal orbits
to the last things: to an unlit city,
an implicit second coming
to the umbra.

FOR JIM DEIGHAN

It was a haven,
a slovenly inroad of the kingdom;
your attic room, your quiet manner.
Afternoons drinking Lapsang Souchong
or nights in Sunderland bars
with my Christ and your agnostic
generous eye for the paradox
I might have crossed
into your half-lit society
had I been less, or more saved.

Those were years between dispensations;
prayer-meetings and drinking sessions.
We lived in no-man's-land.
The night you threw the stalks for me
I thought the devil would have me for it.
Now I follow a Celtic interlace
and find the hexagram of peace.
So much do I owe you.

Where are you now, Jim?
Keeping low beneath a Glasgow night,
smoking in some bedsit
with the knowing fringe?
Or gone to that valley
with its eastern landscape
and magic mushrooms?
Either way, tread easy:
I lift my can of Guinness to you

– and see your figure rise
in a blur of sacred and profane grace
without hangover or judgement
with risk and with the inscape of peace

and pronounce
in love and alcohol
this blessing:

no harm come to you, Jim.
Be full of peace, my brother.

IN MEMORIAM JOHN McGURK

Do the dead mourn the dead,
cradling the tired head,
nursing them from the hurt of the flesh?
In my dreams I see them stoop to wash

grief from the brow of one
I hear them calling 'son'
and 'brother'. Look how gently they have
swabbed clean his slack body, and their grave

kind faces are sorrow's
perfect likenesses; whose
memories are deep with pain, and death
drawn like a blanket to them. With

what patience they have touched
his limbs to warmth, and hushed
the small tremors of his mind. And now
they breathe on him, and say his name. Oh

their voices fall like light
on him, the shadows flit
across his brain. 'John, John,' they say,
'Wake up now.' And he wakes to their day.

HER ROSARY

(*i.m. Mary Armstrong 1916–83*)

Here is her rosary;
five sad mysteries in the hand,
five sorrowful decades
in the breath of a chant.

What hangs in their parabola
is the blue of her skies:
an element of promise,
a gift of healing.

What shows to the eye
is the maculate hand, the skin drawn tight
over a bone frame, sorrow clenched
on a featherweight chain.

To the grieving son
a neutral space;
to the feuding son
a peace-giving.

Here is her rosary, her mother's
before hers, and now
a mesh of links, a fine tether
to hold us.

I SEE MYSELF IN THE WOMB

as the curled frond
        furled amphibian
little berry.

       This hand
is bunched as a white bud,
a soft fist
        shaped in the round cradle.

       This heart
quivers at the ribs: the threaded vessels
      pulse
          on the massive head.

And the soul?
        In the stem
of the neck? The dark bruise
of the eyes?
        In the belly of the mother,
in the coiled tether.

The mind slides on a shift in the stream:
the brow frowns
      over dark water

and to the nub of the ear
the pressure of another's heart, its dense thrum
       like the *hush* of an ocean:

    thrum.
    thrum.
    hush.

Rocked on the full tide, slung
    in a nest of currents:
                              turning inward now

the ear strains
after a heart's gravity:
      the hush
of a going sea.

A SONG FOR THE FAITHFUL DEPARTED AT THE WINTER SOLSTICE

Perpetual light. Light perpetual.

I had seen their faces lifted each in a pool
of light, each in his or her lit cocoon
radiant, and at rest, and alone.

That was death's great temperate basilica.
They kept the offices of silence there.

But now I see them go hand
in hand across this winter's ground

unsure and amazed on their feet,
a tentative company in the low sun's light.

Particular light on particular soil
and the light is perpetual.

A DEAF WOMAN IN HER OLD AGE

She has withdrawn this winter
to her one room, and the house grows numb
as her warped fingers. She is moving ever
inwards now, camped behind the stiff drum,
tensed to an inner ear's
soundings, the brain's singing corridors.

She has become curator of unlived
lives. Turning on her narrow floor
she indicates this vase, that picture. Her loud
sad voice cradles clumsily each memoir,
each intimate grief. And her losses crowd
to her skirts, shy and afraid;

her silenced children, her grieving misfits
who find in this one silence a voice
in her fingers' touch on mine, in light's
threading of her hair. *Hear us*
they whisper, and her grasp petitions
healing: her breath pleads deliverance.

And all her ghosts come walking
from their missed chances, their sad
marriages, all the lives that formed wrong,
but standing upright now, their stiff-knuckled
fingers supple, their children gathered
from their absences, the unreconciled dead

come back to be embraced.

THE RESURRECTION OF THE DEAD

They rise to light, drifting
like pollen over wide fields

where hedges cast no shadow
and loam

shedding itself from them falls
like great crumbs of black bread

to the earth's table.
They are sacramental, a real presence;

the flexed tendon praises, psalm
of muscle, bone of God.

The taut thigh lifts one from his grave.
A print forms in the graveside clay

and he joins these others
walking with purpose

murmuring of hills
generously watered,

of the tree's green sabbath
and of the labour of the tree.

TOLLESBURY

Here the lines are indistinct;
the sky, the sea,
the Essex marshes

where the fleet
once bore the grain
in barges from Old Hall
down to the Blackwater
and the Thames,

where the cowbell clatter
of halliard on mast
rattles against
the wind.

Land peters into sea:
the broad fingering estuaries
dovetail mud.

Wind rises, and shifts

bearing from land
the smoke of stubble.

KEEPING SILENCE

(for Arnold Spector)

'That *is how a picture is attached to reality;
it reaches right out to it.*'
                    Wittgenstein

Deft tendrils brush
the yielding world, like
fingertips on a cheek's
down
      or reach endlessly
towards that face
where no object, no
stiff nugget lies
beneath the blanketing
air, beneath the down
of grasses
      at the eye's corner.

Between mirrors of sky
land's last sliver
edges seaward, inch-deep,
a surface-tension of speech
above deep currents of silence.

Where the estuary gives
to open sea, the voice gives also
and we pass into the life of things
chartless
      asking nothing

speaking no words
but the words
of wind, sea,
      endlessly stretching

A SONG AT FOUR A.M.

*'They were all written about four in the
morning – that still blue almost eternal hour
before cockcrow, before the baby's cry'.*
                              Sylvia Plath

Beyond touch

beyond all measure of healing
this blue membrane, this sky's arctic.

These are the hours of the precise nerve;
each datum immanent as pain,

a world nine parts sky
in the mind's glass,
in the white morning

where I go
with pinpricked fingers
to my daughter's rising

to bring her
into a thin light

the sun's wound spilling
over low storeys

like her cry
on the blank map of morning.

PROMISED LAND

(*i.m. Sibongile Naoni*)

To you who among the congregation
of the faithful remained faithful to the houses
of stone, whose gospel was sun
over grasslands and the sources
of thousand-mile rivers, a nation
coming to birth like prayer answered
where Christ came gathering all the militant dead.

When I heard third-hand of your death
I remembered the picture of your countrywoman
bare-breasted over your bedsit hearth,
her purity of bearing, the clear African
sky behind. And you now one with
all she spoke of, looking past us, your eyes fixed
on another continent, another context

where I see you walking from our low encampments,
casting off our every other notion like
superfluous Western clothes, in the glance
of the sun, in the meek
emerging country; a common inheritance
where we'll meet some day, on your terms, in
the wind's grassland psalm, sunlight's benediction.

A GIFT OF HEALING

(*To Kathleen McCormack*)

A leaf from the tree of grace.
Scurf from the skin of God.

    Should you hear
of the soul's fall, its sound's touch
would be a grief, a wound
you must show God,

baring its stigmata
to the stitch of judgement,
cradling your own wound
under a dark placenta.

    If there is healing
and the earth knit the broken vein

then we might touch
in the warm of the earth; you

who hold the soul's tree straight
beneath the sky
of the word's parchment

and I, who drift on the currents
in the dark
of God's tree:

a membrane of a leaf,
a mind's tissue,
a follower of airs

    whose gift hangs
in the hammock of the air, in
the healing of a sound's touch,

in the kingdom of the ditch:

who brings now
in words you'd grieve to hear
a prayer from the ditch:

    that you tend
the soul's sapling, let fall
the dead leaf;
    that you bend the tree of your body

to the heart's weathers, to
the earth's macula.

    From a high bough
in the growing tree of my grief
look, my sister,

where I grub for the tongue of the root
and the bulb's prophecies.

SILENT ANCESTRY

1

The path clags
underfoot, a snare
of fern, trickster
in the reed-bed.

I have come silent-footed
through firs, on paths
matted with the years'
shed needles

and stand barefooted,
rooted in a small earth,
at an edge, distanced.

2

A Family Portrait

I am cumber-footed
in these sepia ranks:
dark-faced generations
lined before me,

the slow exposure
of mind, silent witnesses.

Men who worked steel,
who crossed from Ireland
sure-footed, Catholic.

3

John McCann's Waistcoat

Unearthed from strata of cloth
almost fossil it comes to light
embroidery twined like lineages
this coat of colours.

Of all the stuff of genealogies,
the plait of branches Jesse dreamt,
their surfaces a patterned coat

a frayed weft of histories
and a seam still firm.